CROSS MY HEART

CROSS MY HEART
POETRY, PROSE ACROSTIC & MORE

GENISE MACE

TATE PUBLISHING
AND ENTERPRISES, LLC

Published by Tate Publishing & Enterprises, LLC
127 E. Trade Center Terrace | Mustang, Oklahoma 73064 USA
1.888.361.9473 | www.tatepublishing.com

Tate Publishing is committed to excellence in the publishing industry. The company reflects the philosophy established by the founders, based on Psalm 68:11,
"The Lord gave the word and great was the company of those who published it."

Book design copyright © 2014 by Tate Publishing, LLC. All rights reserved.
Cover design by Gian philipp Rufin
Interior design by Jomar Ouano
Illustrated by Carolina Carranco & Genise Mace

Published in the United States of America

ISBN: 978-1-62902-369-4
1. Poetry / Women Authors
2. Poetry / Subjects & Themes / General
13.12.21

Contents

Introduction

*Welcome to my world and a little change of thought, sit down
a spell take off your shoes and enjoy this book you've bought.
Let's dive right in get started now and learn what makes me tick,
happy, sad, confusing, funny, there is quite the pick. I've
romanticized, exposed some lies and put it out to past, any
questions left stuck in your head well then all you do is ask.
Reach out to me I'll drop a line maybe a little note. Fan, celebrity,
reporter? Yes! I'll even give a quote. So grab a pen,
Ipad or possibly a phone, I would love to chat I prom,
so look me up my name's Genise; email
Crisscrossmyheart2013@gmail.com*

Through the Authors Eyes

This set of poetry and prose is comprised of works based on dark and lonely times in my life, my feelings about marriage, religion, false friendships, positivity and more.

DARK IS THE NIGHT

Drowned in its untimely blackness, smothered in the dark that
surrounds me
stifled I cannot move.
No light to penetrate even the surface, no will left to break free.
Captured, haunted and forsaken what has happened to me?
The Murky deep I reside in allows no hint or clue,
for no more than fleeting moments of this black water can I see through.
I beg for my release, I pray to be delivered, yet I know that I will die
here
alone with my shaded memories cornered, wilted and
defeated draped in over whelming despair.

The Thirteenth Hour
(Time)

In my darkest day how will it be recalled, how will it be remembered?
The time put in viewed little or great, a sacred task, a service not yet
rendered.
Brought forth to answer a commission that has not been fulfilled,
might I be left standing, or has thy morbid fate been sealed?
An oath left behind, a vow trampled and broken,
A mere thirteen hours wrought, for shame such a pitiful token.
Now endless guilt rest upon my head, for the utterance
set out from me stating "our lord thee, I do wed."

Say What?

Say what! What did you say? No please say that again.
I think I am mistaken because you call yourself my friend.
Repeat what you just said, but say it louder now.
Oh the liberties you're taking, how your mother must be proud!
I dare you to reiterate, put it out there one more time.
Come again, let's hear it, you've already crossed that line.
I see you're on a roll; you're getting it all out,
Why just say what you mean, what's this really all about?
Ha ha! I can't believe you, so you've held it all this time? And for
"that" your crummy friendship could turn on such a dime?
Say What? You call it as you see it and you're gonna speak your mind?
Well loose lips sink ships and now your @$! Is mine!

Forget it

Into everything I've poured my heart, only to find back to the beginning is where I must start. Do I turn and walk away, or should I turn away and run, how do I continue this long journey that I have begun?

When all else fails and my dreams are now long gone, will I look back in regret at those that carried on.

If I give in and wither away, time will tell what lies beyond this day but the path is blocked at every road so forget the things I think I'm owed.

I'll admit defeat and go my way, better luck next time "me" happiness has too high a priced finder's fee.

THE SAD END

so quick it was to get here
So long "it" to begin.
If you ask what do I speak of
I speak our sad end.
All the horrors that surround us
and the pain that's cause by men,
we're fighting a losing battle
every day from deep within.
So quick it was to get here,
so long "it" to begin.
I'll see you on the other side
because this is our sad end.

"IGNORANCE IS BLISS"

I choose not to know, I'd rather just not see,
the world that is unfolding, unraveling before me.
Who am I to listen or keep a clear eye view?
Life is more intriguing when we ponder what we do.
I believe that most are good the majorities alright,
I sleep a soundly slumber and my doors aren't locked at night.
You speak of wars and sorrow and things of future come,]
I say that's for the ignorant not the wealthy lettered one.
All will be fine our world is just evolving there's no culminating end of
which mankind cannot be solving.
So please cut your words and worry of my being from an ado,
I don't foresee events nothing I can't breeze right through.
I'll not submit my person or will to gods not here;
I'll believe it when I see it there's no reason for your fear.
I've done my own fine thinking, I live by My accord,
This message that you speak ask for time I can't afford.

All happens for a reason but we'll be just fine you'll see,
I'm going green, taking Yoga and drinking herbal tea.
There's others' too, they'll come together all pitch in agree,
as this new wave of government brings peace and unity.
So in good time I'll watch I'll wait, and keep the faith in kind,
I believe in karma, Yin and yang AND THE
FATE OF THEIR DESIGN!

Cult Legend

A star in your own right
the master of your domain.
A following of people that
will forever speak your name.
For all of those who know you
not many really do, tucked
away from the world you kept
your heart and you.
Just stepping out enough, to
let a little shine, we be forever
grateful you left your words
behind. Some wanted to be with you
others by your side.
It hurt not only you on the day
you died. So lonely is the world
now that you are not here, at least
some got to know you and their
love for you sincere.

Yesterday's Tomorrow

Today I'll do much better than the
day before. Thinking, trying, striving
more and more and more. A lot to be
accomplished in just so little time,
Oh so many people with troubles
double mine. It seems so hard to
carry, the burden that lies ahead.
Pushing ever onward not knowing where
to tread. Tomorrow will be better
than it was today, I know I can do
something find another way. I'll
pick and choose the moment
to try and make me shine. Only
the odds against me will determine
the design. Yesterday was better than
any time today, every step along the
road feels longer every day. Today I'll
do much better than the day before,
pushing ever forward to find out
what's in store.

The Best of Acrostics

These acrostic poems were written from the heart, based on my sincere admiration for the individuals they were written for.

FOOLS RUSH IN
RICHARD CRISPIN ARMITAGE

Roaming through the past recalling her enchantment as every leaf she
   touched
Intriguing was the snare of his allure, that trapped her with every branch
   she brushed
Caution to the wind she rode, her back fading in the dusk
His hand outstretched to greet her, his eyes are saying much
Arriving in due splendor to his open arms she rushed, majestic the
Reception, her heart overwhelmingly in flux.
Dear that I beseeched you, you came to me at once, and the way he led,
   she followed…

Causing quite the fuss, though at such time not knowing, whose silence they
   shan't trust
Revealing hidden secrets giving all in love and lust, happy were the two
   now free from chains of rust
Indulging, dancing, laughing recognizing only us,
She said and swore her promise to his loving touch, no distance
Placed between them could ever be too much. He gave himself completely
Immersing in the just, holding fast to his fine Lady he asked her hand
   entrust
No man did she so wonder, nor Gent was there in plus, he, her one and
   only, her love forever thus.

Amidst, an evil lurking hiding in the cache, a plot set forth to plunder their
   amorous dreams to dash
Razed to the earth their future, lives gone in a flash
Matchless power brought upon them should they execute the bash, the words
   "come back to me at once!"
Issued to the vast, disloyalty he charged, both deserving of a thrash! In…
Tears she sliced her garment with a blade from tween her sash. "I'll not
   return to him!" she vowed
Accompanying every slash, we'll leave this place and not look back, let him
   burn it all to ash.
Go swiftly; draw your chattels to make way before the clash.
Ever if they find us be our fates much worse than lashed, so forward on
   they went into Sherwood pass.

MESSAGE IN A BOTTLE
MARK A. M.M TURNER

Moving tween the dawn making each day count for much, there was a man
who lived his life but
Always in a rush. "I have no time for wife" he said or "kids to give me grief
"as he boasted of his solitude they looked in disbelief
Relax some cried, settle down just enjoy the show, there is a lovely world to
see if only you let go. "No thank you" he replied I'll
Keep my schedule be, the only break is trouble that's all I'll find in free. But
as he made his way, onto his next design…

Afoot was something vital of which never crossed his mind. The wind it
whistled fiercely & snow covered the shield, the wings began to
Rattle & the storm refused to yield. "Tuck your head down tightly!" yelled a
woman from ahead, & clinging to his satchel he
Accepted every word she said. "It'll be alright you see, don't panic or have
doubt, we've been through this before we always make it out."
Great thunder and loud crashing was all that he now heard, everyone was
silent no one said a word. His bags were laid about him
On seats & on the floor, he watched ever intently as a man reached for the
door. "Don't open it!" he said
Not knowing what to think "have we landed in the water, are we going to
sink?" the door it opened slowly, sand came sliding in

Moisture filled the cabin; a sea breeze was on the wind. "We've hit a beach,
we're stranded!" Called the man from by the door
Much of the day they worked like they never had before, he grabbed his
phone & papers held them as

Tightly as he could, he did what came quite natural what any expert would.
I'll put a call to corporate they'll surely have a plan
Upon hearing our misfortune I know they'll send a man, "The phone it's still
not working, I have somewhere to be!" & the
Reality of the matter was just setting in you see. They thought "We'll make
the most of this, for we may be a while" & just then he
Noticed a woman walking down the aisle. She smiled and worked beside
him as they made the island home, a "heaven" just for them
Emancipated they did roam. He, all clear of fuss & strife he used to know,
till one day a ship passed by and offered them a tow, now…
Repulsive the idea of the life that held him so, he tossed his hands into the air
and decided not to go.

OBVIOUS HEART *GEORGE WEISS

Greatness is bestowed every once in a while to those who will hold it true.
Endeavored to bring about a better life for others you claimed your position.
One can only be grateful that you asked nothing in return.
Restoring in so many, confidences lost through grief or strife.
Giving new hope to a generation lost among a generation lost; with kindness.
Enthusiastically you forge ahead facing every challenge or defeat along the way.

Willingly you are given respect and admiration.
Evidence of your character needs no introduction for actions speak louder than words.
Imparting courage to those in an otherwise discouraging place you have done.
Success will follow all who care to partake of the generous gift.
Surely you will be remembered by all you have touched in such a dear and loving way.

HAVEN
LORALEE WEST

Like the waters of the sea your kindness is abundant.
Outpouring on those you encounter...
Readily and freely giving selflessly.
A lone facet of your many qualities.
Life's true model of a mother and friend;
Encouraging, patient and loyal; always...
Eager to bestow the gift of wisdom.

When a day passes into night, those you've touched think of you.
Each smiling remembering your beauty;
Sentimentally speaking of you to others...
They perpetuate your savoir faire.

ALL THE THINGS SHE SAID
NICOLE BRONSON

*Night fell slow& softly as her face glowed by the fire, I watched her plan
so keenly while she spoke to the man of hire.*

*I will make him disappear, yes go away for quite a while, this burden you
won't bear" he said & gave a quick sly smile.*

*Can you make him suffer, cause him pain for what he's done? I sat
thinking of his torture & highly doubt I'm just "the one."*

*Oh he'll get what's coming, more than his fair share, by the time that I
am finished he'll have grief to give in spare. She …*

*Looked into his eyes & gave him the okay, & with her word & his new
fortune he took his things and went his way*

*Every day that followed I waited for the news, my mind it raced with
questions wondering which method he would use*

*My mother said "don't worry he won't feel a thing, it'll be quick, fast and
in a hurry like when he gave me this here ring." "No…*

*Better is a man, than his word" she told me then, "They spew their
cunning lies as a way to rope you in." She said the*

*Ring it binds you, holds you to their will, but little do they know a
woman's strength can often kill. And just then it happened*

*One knock upon the door, I held my breath completely as mother walked
across the floor. She grabbed it open swiftly*

*Not a second had it passed & as the hired man stepped in, the glass I held
then crashed, he looked right at my mother &*

*Said "it has been done." Her eyes lit in excitement & she whispered "it
has begun" he handed her a package saying*

*Open it & see, then she rubbed her hands together in such a joyful glee, I
rushed myself right over, full of fright & fear*

*No! I said; you didn't! And with a hand touched to her pocket she said
"don't be silly my dear, if you want to hurt a man you have to hit
him here!"*

Fly
Quincy Jones

Quietly we ask "who is he?" Drawn to his essence we ponder.
Utterly entranced we fade, leaving all else behind
Incorporating his passion into our lives day by day
Never losing a beat we step
Captivated by "one" through many, generations to come...
Yesteryear and today, listen.

Judgment rendered, deemed you of honor.
One to be recognized, shadowed and precious.
Noting what you brought, contributed, and shared we bow.
Everlasting words and musical expression flow effortlessly forever
Satisfying us, reminding us and teaching us to fly.

A Virtue
(Edward J McGlinchey)

Every day is a journey one step beyond the day before, but how will it
*   be remembered?*
Disasters round our every hour, but your patience to endure the onslaught
*   is a virtue.*
We fail to see so many times the things that truly matter…
And still we are given more than a second chance.
Reaching beyond what others consider normal is your nature.
Dare I say much more for it would be deemed inappropriate in certain circles,

Just know that no matter how this chapter may come to an end, I have
*   gained more than I will have lost.*

Moreover, new beginnings often come with mistakes and obstacles only
*   in need of a forgiving eye.*
Candidly you speak, and your words uplift, empower and entertain me.
Graciously I accept your advice…
Learning that each road traveled, broadens horizons and opens doors
*   sealed long ago.*
I ask, is it worth it, and the answer remains yes.
Not only in my mind but also in reality, for life has much to offer.
Can I ultimately attain your attentive and selfless quality?
Hopefully that too will come to pass.
Eventually everything does…
Yet you make it appear effortless, and still it brings some burden but
*   hopefully none too much to bear.*

Saddened Heart
Adrien Brody

All too often I'm troubled by the thought of what isn't.
Dreams and fantasies have become my every waking hour.
Reality dawns its unforgiving truth in my mind.
I know that what I feel can never be.
Encountering one such as you, to capture your attention?
Never in a million years could I fathom the possibility.

Broken once again by my hearts foolish desire I lie alone.
Reflecting on what brought me to this point I find loneliness.
Overwhelmed by my emotions I act too hastily.
Drowned in blindness and forgotten with loves demise I wait.
You'll never find me for I am beyond your reach, I do not exist.

FOREVER
DEVON SHOLLENBERGER

Day broke and I came to find you were no longer here with me.
Every moment outside of your presence is a moment wasted.
Vehemently I proclaim my love for you but it falls on deaf ears.
Only time will tell if you feel the same, but we are not guaranteed time.
Never knowing how deep still waters truly run, I took the dive.

My life rest in your capable hands, will they grant me contentment?

Should I succumb to the encroaching lonely end or will you rescue me?
Hell itself dare not keep me from your arms, will they welcome me?
Obstacles stand before us, but none too great for us to conquer.
Little did I know you would steal my heart, but its return is unwanted.
Life without knowing love is no more than an empty existence.
Eventually we all decide to whom & when we devote our affections,
    will it be me?
Nevertheless I'll wait.
Beckoned by your beauty I answered, and then found no escape.
Every minute with you yields a better man than the man the
    minute before.
Revealed are my feelings and the ardor I offer, will you accept it?
Given this day we were not promised I promise; not only in words but
    in actions.
Expectantly I remain in the distance waiting to heed your call, will you
    summon me?
Regardless of the favor in which your adoration settles, our time will be
    forever treasured.

SHADOW OF THE DAY
OTTO SANCHEZ

Observantly I sat quietly waiting
Thinking, trying to come to a decision
Taking every aspect of the situation into account with...'
One moment after another passing by, leaving me just as insecure as the
previous

So I remained in the shadows
Among the others who dared to step forward, eventually
Night fell and still I hadn't approached.
Charmed, yet afraid of your response I discouraged the thoughts,
Having no real basis for my enchantment.
Even so it lingered,
Zealously invading my consciousness at every turn

"IF..."
HANS MATHESON

Hide *your intentions from me but bring close your ear.*
Allow *me one moment of explanation while...*
No *more than a question of nothing more than a glance is....*
Solemnly *told from my heart.*

My *fear is sinking, drowning in an emotional sea that is deep as the*
distance between the heavens and the earth.
Antagonistically *the moon chases me down a lone stretch of highway*
following my every movement.
They *say these things aren't real they say they just can't be, but in your*
eyes within your soul of many things I see....
Honesty, *wisdom, pride and truth...*
Earnestly *displayed in every action and*
Selfishly *I drink, taking more than what will sustain me.*
Offering *remorse for my own measures I lay down my pride.*
Now *nameless, faceless and naked I stand before you experiencing*
your character.

SWAY
CHRISTOPHER MELONI

Clouds move in a motionless sky and the night becomes their only savior.
Heavens lost angels landed near you but your soul remained intact.
Resurrected from the ruins of what once existed you emerged magnificently balanced.
Innocence is something you no longer possess but corrupted you are not.
Silently your loyalties sway, struggling between right and what others deem wrong.
Time brings with it the questions; what is, what could be & what's next.
Openly you declare your feelings for those around you and those closest to you.
Painstakingly you avoid being returned to
Pandora's Box from whence you came.
However, hope remains for any that desire all it has to offer.
Entranced we are pulled into the maze that lies ahead.
Reluctantly some enter while others go blindly and without hesitation.

May god have mercy on our souls as we know not what we do, or its consequences.
Encompassed in a life time of striving is regret as our true purpose is finally revealed.
Long ago the world became twisted and has yet to come untangled.
Only those endowed with inner light can lead the fallen to grace where they belong.
Never again when these days have passed shall we ever be lost in darkness.
I wait for you to deliver me from the chamber I'm so securely held in against my will.

MILLENNIUM
SEAN PATRICK FLANERY

Suddenly you were there at my disposal to cater to my every whim.
Eventually that amenity too would pass.
All along I knew you were much too breathtaking for me to truly obtain.
Now left with the pain of your leaving, I'm buried in my own relentless grief.

Passing time takes an eternity and beyond from hour to hour.
Am I adjusting to the void, black, and massive that draws in the tiniest shred of light?
Trusting secretly is my heart that you will want to return not by request but of free will.
Reluctantly I wait for you,
Imagining your eyes fixed upon me holding me dear in their memory.
Carrying me across the thresh hold of a friendship timeless and ageless.
Kept inside me you will forever be, not wanting to let go.

Flawlessly you expressed regret, its true meaning realized by your actions.
Landing below the hurt yet just above the pain with nothing to cushion the blow I fell.
Against all else I fought, for you, by you, and with you.
Nowhere between this world and the next can anything tear apart what's so tightly woven.
Echoes of your words travel miles to reach my ears at their precise moment.
Restlessly I continue to wait, dreaming of the days before us.
You're here and I welcome you but die in your embrace, awaken me.

YOUR WILL
ORLANDO BLOOM

Our hearts are taken one by one and left behind to wilt.
Reminded of things we'll never possess we gaze, despite the inevitable outcome.
Life and all it has to offer cruelly suggest our paths never cross.
A proposal I will never accept,

Nonetheless the barrier stands between us ever firm and upright.
Drawn by everything that is you, as I see you, but again my wings are singed.
Optimistically I enter once more, though my wounds have yet to heal.

Beautiful mistake to perfect for us to hold
Luring those who dare to drink of your essence forbidden as it is.
Overcome with emotion invoked by your presence we fail to remain dignified.
Orlando you are a gift to many and the smiles you beget will be accounted.
More importantly, you are the reason I...

THE OTHER SIDE
A TRIBUTE TO CHRISTIAN BALE

Crisis befall us all,
Heaven knows the struggles we endure.
Random acts and unforeseen occurrence leave us battered, bruised
and shaken.
I have also suffered.
Seduced we are, into the dark frame of mind…
That one so hard to release.
Ideally we let go
Actually *we harbor, hold on to the pain and…*
Nothing fills the void.

But eventually we mend, find the strength and move forward.
Always looking with our head toward the sky, hoping for tomorrow,
not…
Longing for what we had, but loving what we have.
Experiencing life, its summits, decline and all the glories in between.

IN BALANCE/ AR COMHARDU'/ I BALANSE
DOMINIC H. M. PURCELL

Dust settles on an uncertain mind changing its life view,
Only to find the man that's left behind what once existed.
Much of himself now lost to the consequences of his actions
Injured and tossed about yet knowing his limitations
Never wanting to return to the former way, his life hangs
In the balance, teetering between beyond and forgotten
Commingling the dusk with the dawn.

Having the will to be collected, he's no longer at the

Mercy of his desire, but strives to find balance.

Pursuing a median that's ever so elusive he faces
Unachieved harmony that may be one step away from
Ruin, still he engages with hope
Cautious though he is of what could befall him
Ever closer to a new beginning he presses on
Living the day yet losing the light
Loving what's learned in search of what's right.

No Games
Breaking Benjamin

Born of ultimate inspiration your songs spill forth.
Replacing the void that was left behind with great expression.
Each word leads to a new meaning that is bound for glory.
And engulfs all who listen.
Know that what you have given will forever outweigh what you will receive.
I can never repay you.
Nor those who draw on you for daily motivation.
Grant us what you will and we your loyal fans will ceaselessly wait.

Bystanders witness your entrancing sound and draw close.
Embroidered into our souls your symbol remains.
Never washing away like an emotional tattoo.
Justifiably you will endure when others have faded away.
And when asked why, we will cry out deservedly so.
Moreover it will be apparent.
In other words we love you.
Now and always.

Love is in the Air

A collection of love poems and random feeling tossed on paper.

THE STORM

*Though the winds howl and whistle and the rain tears through trees I
am not frightened.*
Though the sky is black and the air is frigid I am not afraid.
*Though the lamps have burned completely and thunder roars above me
I am not fearful.*
Huddled in my corner you hold me but calmly coax me from it.
Afraid I am, I admit frightened and fearful of the storm.
*Look at me and render it powerless against me, take my fear away
once more.*
Help me as you always, make me fearless of the storm.

THE LONG NIGHT

Not until after I spoke did I realize the impact my words had upon you. The look on your face showed concern and your eyes dawned feeling I didn't know existed. My heart melted for you but I dared not ask you how you felt. I wanted to touch you but I didn't. As you looked at me I saw something I hadn't noticed before, I knew you saw it in me too. How would the night have us end? What did we truly want from one another, more or just passing comfort? I was a flower waiting to bloom from your nurturing and care, yet I sat terrified knowing the slightest emotional frost would make me wither and die.

When you reached for me I ran, I ran as fast as I could only to find I had run into your arms. I stayed there for what seemed to be an eternity though still not long enough. The morning found us in an embrace that I was not willing to end. The pure satisfaction I felt from a simple hug will forever stay with me and I'll always remember that long night.

THE WAY THAT I DO

Can you tell me once again all the things you've said?
I've tried and struggled to remember but the words aren't in my head.
I know you feel the way I do, and that we just won't last.
However I've been thinking about our problems and we should put
them in the past.
Now I'm not one to stick around through the thick and thin,
But what we have is far too great to just say I give in."
You're loving, sweet and kind, too cherished to let go,
And if I haven't told you lately I'll tell you, that I Love You so."

I HOPE YOU FIND

To the things you need and want, to everything you desire.
I hope you get your wish, I hope you find that fire.
A lady ever fair a woman to share your views,
one that you will cherish, a companion, lover & muse.
May she hold you ever tight and in her grace you'll stay,
And may the sorrow you've endured begin to fade away.
The burning of new love yields emotions that flow with ease,
so I hope you find that fire, the maiden within your dreams.

DEAR HEART

Secure in you love for me, you sustain my existence.
Never apart for one moment, I need you and you are there.
Dear heart without you where would I be?

THE SCENARIO

I'd be in a book store or maybe
buying clothes, and our eyes would
meet as my head arose. I'd see you
watching me, from an aisle away, an
encounter such as this could only
happen on today. Your eyes are
looking through me I can feel your
very soul. I'm being drawn to you
by no will of my own. This feeling I
want to fight, the pressure I cannot
stand. My faster beating heart is
awaiting your command. Moving ever closer
with every step you take, I wonder if
this journey I will dare to make.
Our eyes will never break **this** *stare*
that has begun. I know what you are
doing turning the two of us to one.
That sound that I keep hearing very
faintly in my ear, is the whisper of
your voice as you've drawn so near.
The lure of this attraction pulls me
in completely; I feel your presence
inside me, all around me, and beneath me.
Your eyes have pierced the fabric of
my very being, will this be as lasting
as it all now seems? Can this moment
survive when **we** *walk through that door*
or were our paths to cross only in
this store?

COURAGE

You make me strong when I am weak
You give me courage I am complete.
You release my mind you make me whole
You gave me light, I have a goal.
I can never thank you, let you
Know what you have done, just continue in the race
this long lasting run. You made me whole when I was weak
I now have wisdom, I am complete
My soul is free my spirit soars, to this I swear
Forever more
I LOVE YOU

Big Love

Your emotions run through me and I wilt away.
I try, and try and try not to think of you each day.
Some might say I'm crazy, others I'm insane, I don't know but
something deep inside me needs to hear your name.
I look to the day I'll meet you, maybe hold you in the rain, the
day we find the reason for our life and possibly the pain.

LEAVE OUT ALL THE REST

I stray; sometimes I lose sight of you my dream.
When that occurs I'm purposely placed back on track it seems.
The path is kept clear making way for your arrival,
But my continuing love, devotion & perseverance are vital.
Sometimes I stray; I lose sight of you my dream.
So I'll only look forward ne'er left, nor right never off track again.
My eye will be made simple, fixed firmly on you
awaiting the arrival of a love that's overdue.

TORN

An emotion of the same, split apart in two.
Knowing I must leave for I can't be with you
There's pain within my heart at leaving you behind.
for I failed to see the outcome of my indecisiveness mind.
So caught up in the moment I couldn't
think to say.
That wrapped up in your love I could
never stay.
It hurts me more than ever to choose between you two.
I'm not sure that's really something I can ever do.
My feelings are so strong don't want to let you go.
But there are luckless words that one of you should know.
My soul, my heart, my love, will always
have been true.
I'm being ripped apart by the thought of losing you.
A decision of this measure will take some
time to make.
This situation we are in I didn't set out to create.
I love the both of you; and I ask that you forgive me,
for leaving one of two well, that can never ever be.

In The Arms of Evil

In the arms of evil is where you right now lay.
In the arms of evil I fear that you will stay.
Held captive by a dragon; the one that I must slay
I know I must release you with my blood if I must pay.
I'll find you twix the smoke and fog, and in between the grey
My faithful love will guide me forth and light the murky way.
On my honor I will save you if I sincerely pray,
all for one or nothing be it come what may
To have you for forever is to hold you for today.
A precious life we'll share together with these three words I'll say...

THE LETTER
DEAR...

By the time you read this I'll already be at my destination. I left because too much has happened between us for me to stay here and be happy. The decision to leave didn't come easily and it wasn't an overnight choice. I wish things could be how they were when we first met. Even now as I sit here writing you this letter I reminisce about our time together. I ask myself if I'd known how things would end would I still love you. Would I still venture down the road knowing the outcome? Would I risk certain heartache to be with you again? Unfortunately for me the answer is yes, I would do it all again causing myself unquestionable pain. Then why have I left, you ask, why am I not standing before you? I've left because if I had stayed we could never recapture what we once had. I believe we came together because much like the light and the darkness you can't have one without the other, however something happened along the way causing us to forget. What my departing has given us is hope; so if you want me you'll find me. No one knows where I am, I'm someplace I've never spoken of not even in passing. If what we had was real I know I'll see you again, until that time take care of yourself and know that I love you.

ADMIRATION

*The Randomness of a picture, and the way it settles in your mind
brings memories that have yet to be made. The feeling that lingers
from moment to moment but fades in the light hours returns at will
when called upon by those who possess it. To outline the curves of your
face from afar, to search your eyes even from a distance is blissful.
Your hair moves in the gentle breeze as if reaching out to touch us.
Sincerity and depth emanate from within for all to see and will
carry you forth to places only imagined on dark and silent nights*

A Little Humor

Silly poems & prose meant to make you laugh.

SAD BUT TRUE

Yes I know it's sad, but unfortunately it's true,
I say there's something wrong with everything I do.
I try to make things work, but they just don't turn out right,
I'm pretty sure that's why I sleep alone at night.
I fumble, fidget, fall so helplessly downstairs, I surely am for certain
That even god won't hear my prayers.
Yes I know it's sad, but unfortunately it's true, so
you *should be glad that I am "me" not "you."*

THE OLD MAN

He pushed and pulled and hollered, kicking and screaming he went.
They grabbed him by his arms and legs, and to the chapel he was sent.
Patiently waiting was his bride to be, with her eyes
fixed firmly on him, he couldn't help but see, a woman
he no longer loved and he wanted to be free.

WHAT IS WRONG WITH ME?

What is wrong with me you asked, I say I do not know, but
let's go back, rewind and then I'll tell you so.
"Please do me a favor, go and change your shoes you
seem to be quite tall and it's giving me the blues.
You have me by three inches, your height is quite extreme, if you
slip on a pair of flats you'll be the woman of my dreams.
I'll engage you in conversation as **we** *take in some art,*
look at that it's time for lunch but don't order from ***that***
cart. I can't afford big meals, my money is very tight just
keep it simple will you and please eat very light.
I don't have much money, fourteen dollars to be exact, so keep
it under seven bucks because I'm sure there will be tax."
You asked "What is wrong with me" well here's my answer true; the
answer is "What's wrong with me?" for wasting time with you!

GRAMS ALWAYS LISTENING

She sits so silent ever yet so still,
when no one cares to give an ear gram always will.
There was one night many years ago I had a story to tell,
Gram snug in her chair poised to listen ready for me to go.
I started in pouring out my soul, rambling on and on,
she never spoke not a single word she only listened as I roared.
After minutes of my ranting, the room still quiet and dark,
I longed to hear grams ideas I waited for her remark.
A minute passed as I watched her eyes so clear and ever sharp, she
stared straight ahead and I got ready cause she was in deep thought.
The minutes passed still no word from gram as the tv rattled
on, 10 minutes down hey this is strange the time has really
gone. I moved in closer and saw her eyes as shiny as can be; they
had been closed the entire time reflecting light from the tv.

But that's another story

On an unrelated note...
The Sleep In Between

The moon moved through the sky, and every living creature could hear a low pitch noise. The sound grew louder and sharper as the eclipse drew closer, and she knew it was time to leave. Minute by minute the sky became darker, and the previous panic in the streets faded as people stood looking up towards the sky. As the event drew closer to totality the ground began to tremble, and she told Luke she loved him. His eyes watered, and he looked at her in a way that said everything he no longer had time to say. She walked away from him and into the street where the shadow of the eclipse fell directly on her. She stood; scared not knowing what to expect, but ready to accept anything bestowed upon her. The darkness began to feel as hot as fire, and it seared her flesh and burned her ears. Seconds later all went silent, and the ground began to shake furiously. The intense light of the corona shined onto the ground where she stood cutting its way to the core of the earth, and she fell in when the earth gave way. She heard fractions of her own screams through the thunderous tearing that surrounded her. As she fell her body felt as though it was being stretched beyond its limits. Everything around her became black, and she realized her sight had been taken from her. At a point, she was suspended in a void, and she hung there horrified and freezing yet burning up. A sound resonated from below her and above her at once, a sound that was later revealed to be a voice. No, more than a voice, it was an unimaginable tone that could never be duplicated by man or machine. It assessed her and her biggest fear had now become her reality. She was standing before him, and it was no longer man's Day of Judgment it was hers and hers alone. As her sight came back to her, she watched every moment she'd ever lived happen before her eyes.

At times, she felt his anger grow towards her for the things she'd done, but then she felt forgiveness. She wanted to speak, but her voice had been taken from her. The time to answer for her actions were upon her, and the only one she was truly held accountable for was her disobedience, the first sin. After she saw all the pain she had caused, again her sight was taken from her, so she readied herself for the final blow knowing whole-heartedly she deserved it. She cried in the void unable to speak, see or hear while an enormous pressure bore down on her until she felt it, the ability to speak had been returned to her, and she spoke the words, and they entered the air in their purest form. רעטצמ -ינא *"I'm Sorry" she uttered and again she began to fall, and when her eyes opened she saw him staring down at her with an expression she'd seen before. He helped her to her feet and guided her by the hand into the woods. There was no fear or hesitation in her steps, she followed him as he showed her all of the beauty that surrounded them. As they walked, various animals roamed about, and from the corner of her eye she saw the serpent making the same journey around the garden. This time with consciousness of mind she ignored it as it slithered about following her every step. Having the only recollection of what happened prior to the moment, she knew in her heart that she would never stray. Vowed to keep her pledge of making right what she had destroyed she held his hand tighter; and as they walked she listened carefully to every word that fell from his lips.*